Microcosm Publishing is Portland's most diversified publishing house and distributor with a focus on the colorful, authentic, and empowering. Our books and zines have put your power in your hands since 1996, equipping readers to make positive changes in their lives and in the world around them. Microcosm emphasizes skill-building, showing hidden histories, and fostering creativity through challenging conventional publishing wisdom with books and bookettes about DIY skills, food, bicycling, gender, self-care, and social justice. What was once a distro and record label started by Joe Biel in a drafty bedroom was determined to be *Publishers Weekly*'s fastest-growing publisher of 2022 and has become among the oldest independent publishing houses in Portland, OR, and Cleveland, OH. We are a politically moderate, centrist publisher in a world that has inched to the right for the past 80 years.

in this issue:

vision42

the architecture of the automobile

london's smart step

cartoons, etc.

vision42

Roxanne Warren, author of The Urban Oasis, *recently participated in an email interview with GBB. With George Haikalis, she founded Vision42, an organization which is attempting to bring a pedestrian- and lightrail-only mall to the most congested street in Manhattan, 42nd.*

The implementation of lightrail on 42nd street would be a strong step towards superseding the personal automobile altogether in urban settings. It would show the literal and symbolic emergence, or more accurately the reemergence, of a community-based and sensible form of transportation in an environment where cars are in fact counterproductive.

Visit **www.vision42.org** for more information.

(GBB) *In the eyes of vision42, what would be your ultimate goal for 42nd Street?*

(Roxanne Warren) We have, basically, several ultimate goals - In addition to providing a vast improvement to NYC residents, employees and tourists in Midtown Manhattan, and giving a much-needed boost to the City's economy, vision42 aims to counter the anti-urban biases that are so prevalent in this country, by demonstrating how desirable cities can be as an alternative to resource-sucking suburban sprawl. This project would combine a densely scaled and a culturally vibrant urban place with high-quality landscaping and high-quality surface transit. It would convert the scale of NYC's most populous street from the automotive scale, back down to human scale -- creating an outdoor "urban room", wherein the pedestrian has primacy.

Give us a brief history of vision42's ability to survive as a political force. Is it part grassroots and part business supported?

This is an effort led by myself, an architect and author, and George Haikalis, a civil engineer and transportation planner, and is an outgrowth of earlier efforts in which we both aided the initiator of a 42nd Street light rail proposal 10 years ago, which was approved by the City Council by a vote of 49 to 2, but was stifled by the then-incoming mayor, Rudolph Guiliani. That proposal would have provided an important improvement to public transit but was not for an auto-free street and made no improvements to the walking environment. George and I have been working for more that 4 years on this version, and have been joined by a wonderful working group of volunteers, who meet monthly and contribute valuable ideas, are making computer drawings, and have constructed our website, www.vision42.org. We have received support from a number of elected officials, and are joined by a distinguished Advisory Committee, which includes seven transportation experts, two of whom are former DOT Commissioner. We've also received several grants from real estate developers, who realize the potential economic boost this would give to Midtown, and have recently received a significant matching funds grant, specifically earmarked for technical studies of the economic and traffic impacts and an updated cost estimate. We have made 126 presentations to date, to a wide range of individuals and groups (see our website), to overwhelmingly positive responses. However, we have still been unable to convince the Mayor, or, more to the point, his Deputy Mayor for Economic Development and Rebuilding, to include a study of vision42 within the Scope of a $41 million study currently being performed for the extension of the #7 subway line to a stadium that they want to build on Manhattan's West Side. This is why we feel compelled to raise money to commission these studies ourselves.

What were the main goals of the founders of vision42, to enhance community, promote business, make the streets safer, attract tourists? Etc..?

(See above.) The greater safety of pedestrians from motorists is obvious; furthermore, security against any terrorist attacks will be greatly enhanced without trucks and cars on the street in busy hours. In any case, part of the eastern end of 42nd Street is closed off to traffic by sanitation trucks when the UN is in session, for this very reason. Potted plants and other landscaping would create a more civilized urban experience than sand-filled sanitation trucks. Additionally, tourists and residents alike typically enjoy traveling by light rail. It's a very civilized way of moving through a city.

Oftentimes in bicycle advocacy, the "business community," for various reasons, wields its power to block bicycle friendly environments. I notice on your site that the business community is actually helping to work towards the goal you have by making contributions. Granted, they have something to gain from it, but have you seen any opposition from any sector of the business community or other special interest groups? Who has put up the most opposition?

We fully expect opposition from the parking garage owners, the taxi industry, the bus industry, theoreticians who don't believe that pedestrian streets work in the US, and any individuals, including city officials, who believe it's a travesty to take street space away from automobiles. We intend to deal with the taxi and bus industries by approaching them early, and asking them "how we could make this work for them". We intend to deal with the automobile champions by going directly to the public with a leafleting campaign. Please wish us luck.

If it comes to fruition (and some of this is probably still up in the air), how will the project be funded?

The vision42 plan, even including high-quality landscaping and pedestrian amenities, is roughly estimated to cost around $200 million, or one-tenth of the cost of an extension to the #7 subway, which is being promoted by NYC's Deputy Mayor for Economic Development and Rebuilding. It could also be completed approximately twice as fast, and in time for the Olympics 2012, if NYC should succeed in its bid. While $200 million sounds like a lot of money, it's not a lot for the high-quality service it would provide, and the improvements in business and property values it would generate. It should qualify well for federal funding, as a cost-effective, environmentally compatible, ADA handicapped-accessible distributor among the ferries, subways, and major transportation terminals in Midtown Manhattan.

What arguments have you found to be most useful in convincing diverse segments of the community that a car-free environment will be a good thing?

We just show them our presentation, containing images of how it's been done all over the world, and photomontages of how it might look on 42nd Street. We also discuss the benefits that have been experienced elsewhere in the concrete terms of increased retail sales and real estate property values.

Would there be anyone who would be adversely affected by your vision of 42nd street?

The parking garage industry, which doesn't belong on 42nd Street anyway. The taxi drivers could drop their passengers off on the north/south avenues, the longest walk from which would be 400 feet. Possibly some of the suburbanites would come into the theater in charter buses and like to be dropped off at the doors of theaters, are totally unfamiliar with using transit, and would object to mingling with the crowds might be deterred from coming into the City at all. On the other hand,, adequate positive publicity, with photos of what it will look like, might have the opposite effect.

Does your vision of 42nd Street stop there, or do you have plans to further promote car-free environments in Manhattan if and when vision42 is completed?

Good question. There are two parts to this issue - the light rail and the auto-free, landscaped aspect. We think that a logical first expansion of the lightrail itself would be across 34th Street, which would create a two-way loop across Midtown. Probably most of 34th Street would initially not be auto-free, except in the area around Macy's. But the success of the auto-free portions of both 42nd Street and 34th Street would be likely to encourage the spread of this concept. This is what happened in the City of Florence: initially merchants opposed a 40-block auto-free zone, until it was implemented, after which merchants were pressing to have it enlarged to include them. There are numerous other possibilities for expanding the vision thing -- for example to the far western and far eastern north/south avenues, which are not served by the subways. But it would be a mistake to try to diffuse our focus right now. We have to bring the public -- and even more so, the City officials (who have been more of a problem, to date) -- around to the revolutionary concept of taking street space away from cars. After all, in can be done anywhere in the US, it should be do-able in Manhattan, where only 23 percent of the households even own a car.

Do bicycles find a place in your plan?

Another good question. There is a problem of space: 42nd Street is only 100 feet wide, building face to building face. I'm attaching a section through a typical block. It has a bar scale, which shows that, if you include outdoor cafes and restaurants, there are only about 15 feet left for strolling and emergency vehicles. Finding space for a bike lane will be difficult. I say this as an avid biker, who until a few years ago rode my bike to the office whenever possible. One solution, which they are using in Minneapolis on the new Hiawatha Line Rail Line, is to include bike racks on the light rail vehicles themselves. We now have a wonderful bike path along the Hudson River, and another developing along the East River, and it would be a shame not to include provisions for bicyclists within this crosstown oasis.

Manhattan is obviously a very densely populated area. Portland, Oregon is less so. In your studies, have you seen anything showing how public transit, specifically in the form of lightrail, actually is cost effective in the long run as compared to personal automobiles?

We are about to commission an economic study which should help quantify its cost-effectiveness. The thing that induced me, as an architect, to study public transit systems in the first place, was that I was appalled to realize how much space was being consumed by automobiles in cities. Each car requires some 350 square feet of space just for parking, even before its circulation space is counted. This is why liberal provisions for cars in cities are antithetical to the whole concept of dense but livable urban space. As far as SUVs in Manhattan are concerned, they are dangerous to and thoroughly resented by both pedestrians and bicyclists; this doesn't need a study -- it's too obvious, and proven by the accident statistics. The SUV drivers are sitting up so high that they can't even see the lowly pedestrian, and certainly don't respect the bicyclists, either. They do <u>not</u> belong in <u>any</u> city.

Do any members of vision42 stand to gain financially, through career advancement or direct donations, if the plan is adopted, or is this purely a move to improve public space?

Promoting this concept is a labor of love, that has been, and continues to be, a money-sucking enterprise. We have received some help from real estate developers who stand to gain from the plan, but we have only gone to them because it is a potential way to get to the Mayor.

Thanks very much for your time, Roxanne. If you have any closing thoughts, feel free to write them here.

You're most welcome, Scott. We very much appreciate your interest and support.

the architecture of the automobile

No invention has done more to destroy urban space than the automobile. For evidence of this, one only needs to step outside one's front door and take a look around with a skeptical eye, especially if the "neighborhood" was planned and constructed post World War II.

Because it is familiar to me, I'll do a quick rundown of my own environment where I currently live, which is actually less car oriented than most places in the United States.

First off, the building itself. I live in a five story apartment building with around 120 apartments. The first floor is entirely parking save the entryway and office and a sandwich shop at one end. The total ratio of parking to non-parking on the first floor is about 5/1 or maybe even 6/1. In order to attract tenants, the developer and owner put in parking on nearly the entire first floor, and in truth it's really hard to blame them for doing so. Many who look for apartments put it high on their list whether or not there is easy parking, so in order to make the place attractive, ample parking has become a sort of reflex for developers.

However, if you can envision it differently, a whole new world opens up. The reason that many need cars is to be able to go and get what they want and need and bring it home. It would seem to make more sense to bring what people want to them, and bypass the entire step of every single person needing to go somewhere to get what they need. For example, if instead of parking occupying nearly the entire first floor, you had a medium sized grocery store, two restaurants, a hardware store and a video rental store, that would greatly reduce the number of trips necessary via personal automobile. For the owner this would fetch far more rent than parking, and if the potential residents could get by without the need of having their cars handy at all times, the building would be much more attractive, not to mention encourage a healthy economic and social center. But the developers and owners more often than not play it safe, or perhaps even make decisions habitually, and like I said it's hard to blame them. They are after all just looking out for their own interests. If the owner, developer and potential residents were all able to see the forest from the trees, that's when a positive change may occur with everyone working together. (This is similar to how opponents of smart growth resist its implementation, stating that residential property will become unaffordable to people because areas where cities build with smart growth in mind typically have higher prices than non-smart growth areas. These same opponents don't consider *why* the prices are higher. Quite simply, it's because more people want to live there, so the demand is greater which drives up the price. Why do people want to live there? Because it's such a nice place to live. Walk to shopping, lively street life, safe for children, a healthy social fabric, etc. This type of resistance to sensible planning encourages the status quo and a continued isolationism and dependence on the personal automobile. There is a reason why there are so many bitter jokes and anecdotes about suburbia. It is a petri dish for boredom and angst, especially for those too old or young to drive.)

Next to my apartment building is a parking lot for high school students, which is filled during school hours, and more or less empty during non-school hours. This is obviously a huge waste of urban space, with it only being "used" about half the day. Again, imagine the vibrant social and economic life if it was instead filled with shops and restaurants. Along with this, it seems ludicrous to have a school that is not within easy and safe walking or bicycling distance for the students, whether they are in the 2nd grade or seniors in college. Why put a district-based institution of any kind where people must drive to get there? It is possible that some students could bike there but decide to drive because it is perceived to be more mature and/or cool, which is another issue. But take away the parking lot, encourage bicycling, and the bikes will come out in full force as happens in Holland and Germany.

Next to the high school parking lot is another parking lot with office building, with a ratio of about

3/1. Similar to the high school parking lot, this space could be used so much more efficiently if it were not allocated for parking. As it is, the people who work in this building have about two choices for walking to get lunch. A sandwich shop across the street and a sandwich shop down the street. This area has the potential of being used all day and all evening, whereas the parking lot is only "used" from nine to five, and then abandoned. There is something just plain idiotic about people having to work a great distance from where they live. When I ponder someone having to drive 20 miles to sit in a cubicle for eight hours a day, it gives me certainty that something has gone terribly wrong with the way we planned our cities post World War II.

Across the street is another office building, also with parking on the ground level. But with this office building, the offices are on stilts above the parking spaces, creating a sort of cave-like atmosphere on the ground level. Not a fun place to walk around, because except for the brightest of days at the right times of day it is dark and there are cars moving around. Next to this building is a traditional lot, just parking spaces with no structures, and it is unclear what this lot is for because it is usually close to or totally empty, another total waste of space, needless to say.

Further on, in order to get to the next neighborhood you must cross a freeway bridge over I-84. I'd be willing to bet that a good 99% of the population would say that it is an unpleasant experience walking over a freeway bridge of any kind. What placing the freeway here did in essence was to create a pedestrian barrier (though you can cross, most would choose not to) in the name of increased auto-mobility, which is ironic considering that at least 4 hours of the day traffic isn't moving more than ten or fifteen miles an hour. A good answer would be to put in more highspeed lightrail that stopped at every exit which would save space, time and indeed money and resources. As with transit ridership, there is a Catch-22 here. Until you make it easy to leave their cars at home, people won't, and until you have increased bus ridership you can't justify the funding. What it will take to get more cars off the road and a shift in both transportation policy and implementation is a mass movement (no pun intended) among residents who are able to envision the advantages and indeed pleasantries of a non-automobile based system.

South of the building I live in lies Sandy Boulevard, a major thoroughfare running East-West on a slight diagonal across Portland's East side. Sandy is a battleground for pedestrians, so much so that it is rare to see any at all except when the Boulevard passes through the Hollywood district where there is a healthy mix of multi-use development and a density that is conducive to the pedestrians. Sandy Boulevard, like the freeway example, works to establish an inhospitable dividing line for those traveling by foot or bicycle, which isolates things and people on the North from things and people on the South (even when traveling by car one is likely to think unkindly of the North-South divide of Sandy). Granted, the street is crossed all the time, but the wait for the light to change can be excruciating when on foot, and because it is so dominated by cars it would be unwise to cross against the light. Crossing even with the light can be a daunting experience, because most cars know it as a high speed road and typically don't expect to encounter bikes or peds. Sandy also has quite a number of car dealerships, which are really little more than parking lots themselves. Get rid of the need for cars, and then you replace those dealerships with businesses that people in the area will frequent, making it a vibrant and healthy place to go. Put in lightrail that goes straight down the Boulevard and runs every few minutes and you would have an oasis that would indeed do wonders for the businesses. With the ability to run straight into downtown (provided the Burnside Bridge could be adapted), lightrail on Sandy would be put to good use. All along it there is housing on either side, and to walk or bicycle to Sandy to catch the lightrail would be intuitive because it's such a main route. Build it and they will come.

Post World War II, city planning took a radical turn for the worse when suburbs and sprawl became the no-brainer style of building (ultra-low density, car-dependent), much influenced by the self-interest of the dominant corporations of the time. Everyone who came home from the war was given the promise of the new "American Dream," a two car garage, a television and a nice big back- and frontyard. Granted, no other country could ever come up with the money to house its citizens this way, but anyone who has ever lived in sprawl knows the boredom and isolationism it creates, which in turn produces television junkies and self-absorbed neurotics.

In any hierarchical society, it is the powers that be who decide how the workers will live (basically the lower 80 percent or so) and those in control never make these decisions lightly. There is a lot riding on them. In the former Soviet Union, the elites did not fear density as it is in the United States. Density by its very nature promotes communication and district-autonomy, but the leadership does not fear that in a totalitarian society because the rules are very clearly defined. Dissent and you'll get what's good for you. This is why the Soviets build what were called in East Germany *Arbeiterschlissfacher*, literally "places to put the workers." These simple and cheap buildings invaded every part of Soviet territory as a pragmatic solution to housing. Rather fittingly, it was designed with "community" in mind, but with the bludgeon hanging over their heads, no true communities developed.

In democracies, methods of control are much more subtle. Because the secret police is not nearly as widespread as in a totalitarian society, one way to control the population is to keep them completely isolated from one another so that any organization is difficult or impossible. To compliment this, you encourage watching television which has frequent news stories about how dangerous and disturbing a world it is out there is, thereby encouraging people not to trust one another and stay home and stay unorganized. The crime rate in the United States is roughly the same as the crime rate in other industrialized nations, yet the fear of crime in the United States is off the scale. This fear is one major way in which the elite class in the United States breeds submission among the lower 80 percent, often playing one race against another so as to distract them from those who are actually pulling the strings and making decisions for them about their lives.

This translates perfectly into the suburban way of life. Isolationism, fear and a feeling of utter powerlessness and disenfranchisement. If we wish to make our own decisions about our own destinies (social, political and economic), probably the best way would not be to make a direct hit against the powerful, but to participate in local politics to encourage smart growth and new urbanism, thereby putting a stop to sprawl and an auto-based way of life.

Watching the early General Motors and Ford propaganda films is telling. They are absolute masterpieces of how to manipulate and control public opinion and identity. A threat to the automobile is indeed a threat to America, and to all the things that make this country great. These films have a certain insidious power along the lines of a cult leader. All effective propaganda, just like all effective cult leaders, appeal to and manipulate emotions which proves to be dangerous.

So we have to ask ourselves; Do we want to live in isolation and fear within the architecture of the automobile? Or do we want to transform our cities into vibrant and healthy places for interaction, creativity and self-determination?

The essence of democracy is participation in your own fate. Without the ability to determine your own fate, you might as well be living in a totalitarian country with secret police and all. At least that way there are no illusions. You know you're a slave, end of story. If you live in a democracy but do not participate in your own social, political and economic fate *and* you claim to be free, then you truly are living a lie.

london's smart step

In order to make central London less of a jungle, a fee was put in place for anyone who entered central city via personal automobile. Though some critics said that this was just a way to make things more tolerable for the rich (because they are better able to afford the fee), money taken in goes towards improving transit which will benefit all who use it and, as the report indicates, improves London in other ways such as improved air quality, improved safety and less noise. Following find a report from Transport for London, *an organization that oversees and manages all things transport related for England's capitol.*

Congestion Charging – February 2004

Since the introduction of the congestion charging scheme in central London on 17 February 2003, congestion has reduced significantly; London's bus capacity has increased and journey times for all vehicles are faster and more reliable.

The primary aim of the scheme was to reduce traffic congestion in and around the charging zone, and so directly contributes to the Mayor's priorities for transport as set out in his Transport Strategy published in July 2001.

Transport for London's February 2004 congestion charging monitoring update provides the latest information on the operation and enforcement of the scheme and its effects on traffic levels, congestion, public transport and business and social impacts.

The report illustrates that the successes and trends outlined in Congestion Charging: 6 months on continue to benefit London.

Key Findings

- Traffic delays inside the charging zone remain 30 percent lower than before charging was introduced.
- Estimates of year-on-year changes in traffic levels during charging hours show a reduction of 18 percent in traffic entering the zone during charging hours, with a reduction of 30% in cars
- Buses continue to demonstrate significant gains in reliability in and around the charging zone, experiencing up to a 60 percent reduction in disruption caused by traffic delays.
- Public transport continues to cope well with ex-car users. There has been a year-on-year increase of 29,000 bus passengers entering the zone during the morning peak period
- There remains no evidence of any significant adverse traffic impacts from the charge as confirmed by latest measurements of traffic volumes in and around the charging zone
- When asked if the business supports congestion charging as long as there is continued investment in public transport, around 60 percent of the surveyed businesses agreed; around 20 percent of businesses disagreed and 20 percent with no change or don't know
- Following the supplemental agreement of September 2003 with Capita (the main contractors operating the scheme) a phased programme of IT, process, management, training and staffing improvements is being progressed and is already delivery improvements to congestion charging customers.
- Following improvements to the enforcement service, the number of Penalty Charge Notices (PCNs) issued average some 165,000 per month
- Representations made in response to PCNs has fallen from 64 percent in the early weeks of the scheme to a recent level of about 22 percent.
- Congestion charging contributes £50 million of net transport benefits to London's

economy per year, mainly through quicker and more reliable journeys for road and bus users.

Reduced Traffic Levels and Congestion

The congestion charging scheme continues to achieve its main objective by cutting congestion within the zone by an average of 30%. The year-on-year reduction in potentially chargeable vehicles (cars, vans and lorries, not including taxis, buses and coaches) is 27%. Cars have reduced by 30%.

Transport for London's congestion charging February monitoring update reports a continuation of the patterns that were established in the first few weeks of the scheme. Payment levels remain relatively constant with some 110,000 payments per day. TfL's Autumn 2003 traffic counts suggest that there has been a year-on-year reduction of 65,000 fewer car movements into or through the charging zone, comparable to the earlier estimates.

Traffic delays have been reduced and the increased public transport capacity is successfully accommodating new bus passengers. Whilst car movements have reduced, taxi, bus and coach movements have increased by 20%. The increase in bus movements largely reflects the additional bus service provision introduced by TfL.

There has been a year-on-year increase of 29,000 bus passengers entering the zone during the morning peak period (07.00 to 10.00), carried by an additional 560 bus trips.

Improvements to bus reliability and journey times reported previously continue to be observed, with the greatest improvements being in and around the charging zone. The additional wait time at bus stops experienced by passengers caused by service irregularity or missing buses has improved by 20% across London and over 30% in and around the charging zone compared to last year.

Bus routes serving the charging zone experience 60% less disruption due to traffic delay.

Whilst there is evidence of some small changes in orbital traffic as predicted outside of the charging zone there is no evidence of significant increases beyond the inner ring road.

Transport for London's Business Surveys

Transport for London carried out interview surveys of over 700 businesses in and immediately around the charging zone during October/November 2003. These can be compared to similar surveys conducted at the same time during 2002.

When asked if the business supports congestion charging as long as there is continued investment in public transport, around 60 percent of the surveyed businesses agreed; around 20 percent of businesses disagreed and 20 percent with no change or don't know

Central London businesses were adversely affected by a number of factors in 2003. These included, first and foremost the general economic slowdown in London last year, a fall in the number of tourists and other visitors to the city, various seasonal factors and the closure of the Central Line during the first part of 2003.

National statistics show that spending by overseas visitors in London was £100 million lower in the second quarter of 2003 compared to the second quarter of 2002, one quarter of which might be retail spend.

The scale of 'financial' impacts of charging on central London's businesses is comparatively small, and broadly neutral in terms of the Greater London economy. There is some recent indication that the impact of these factors is starting to wane, and that the relevant indicators are returning to their long-term trends.

Improvements to Operations

Most aspects of the operation of the congestion charging scheme have been functioning satisfactorily since charging commenced. However, TfL's monitoring and chargepayer feedback on the first months of operation highlighted concerns around some aspects of the service.

In August 2003 changes were agreed to TfL's contract with Capita. Capita has invested substantially to provide an enhanced level of service to central London congestion charge users.

Capita's first two milestones were met in October 2003 and January 2004. The full programme of improvements is due to be completed by the end of March 2004.

Enquiries via the call centre average around 70,000 calls per week, falling from the 167,000 average of the first few weeks of operation. Significant reductions have been observed in the waiting times and average call times.

Enforcement

The percentage of recovered Penalty Charge Notices and payment levels have steadily increased since the start of the scheme. For PCNs issued in September 2003, 70 percent have been paid.

Payment and compliance levels are expected to increase further over time, as those who have been issued PCNs recognise that the enforcement process is effective and that unpaid PCNs will be actively pursued.

There has been a significant reduction, month on month, in the number of representations made by vehicle keepers in response to PCNs. The proportion of PCNs against which representations are made has fallen from 64 percent in the early weeks of the scheme to the more recent level of about 22 percent. This indicates both increased familiarity with the scheme and improvements in the operational systems.

Whereas in the first months of operation the main reasons for representations were as a result of Capita or chargepayer data entry errors, such as an incorrect vehicle registration number, the majority of representations currently being received are made by vehicle hire companies, informing TfL of the correct driver details of the vehicle hirer on the day the charge was not paid.

Around 2% of all PCN's issued were appealed of which 57% were found in favour of TfL. Only 4% of PCN's issued have not been paid and had warrants of execution issued to bailiffs. 255 persistent evaders (drivers with three or more unpaid PCNs) have had their vehicle clamped or removed by TfL.

Summary

London's congestion charging scheme continues to effectively reduce congestion, improve bus and car journey times and help improve London and its environment. TfL will continue to monitor its impacts closely to ensure that these benefits are maintained.

letters from the front lines

Fund TriMet, help limit cars *(published in* The Portland Tribune *in Feb., '04)*

Fred Nussbaum's letter covers important issues concerning TriMet (*TriMet needs to toughen up,* Insight, Jan. 23). If we are to limit the use of the single occupancy automobile (as the city of Portland's Transportation System Plan advocates), TriMet needs to implement no-nonsense, pragmatic solutions so more commuters can depend on service regardless of weather conditions.

That said, however, I think TriMet did an outstanding job considering this was the worst storm in decades. All the cities mentioned in Nussbaum's letter -- Denver, Salt Lake City and Minneapolis -- are well prepared to deal with extreme weather because they confront it yearly. It would be expected that they could tackle them with relative ease, whereas Portland must roll with the punches, to a degree, when an extraordinary storm befalls us.

Because oil is a scarce commodity, and because it's impossible to produce it once it runs out, public transit will have to step in when peak oil production is reached (estimated to be sometime between 2010 and 2020). The sooner we start building more MAX lines and bicycle routes, the better off we will be. Nussbaum's letter addresses how the loss of service during the storm affected people who have no option other than public transit. One way for them to protect their interests, while making the city safer and more livable, is to make sure the city knows that funding TriMet is more important than the prolongation of car culture, which is inferior in nearly every way.

Scott Larkin
Northeast Portland

email from china

Dear sir:

We fetch you E-Mail address from internet.

We are a very large manufactory in Chongqing of China. We can supply electrical scooter, electrical trip jeep or bus. And CNG series tricycle, 4 wheels taxi motorcycle-car, from 150cc to 650cc Engine.

I am very glad to write the email to you, we hope to cooperate with you, at present, our factory manufacture CNG DB175 motorcycle-car stock for supply, thus We could send the shipment within 20 days, when we receive your T/T or origin L/C. the minimum order quantity is one 40' container.

Please you receive detail picture in accessory.

1, Electrical scooter(electrical motorcycle). electrical cycle, electrical trip jeep golf car and bus.
2, CNG series tricycle, 4 wheels taxi motorcycle-car, from 150cc to 650cc Engine.
3, Two-wheel motorcycle(had 4 type pass CE-2)
4, ATV ,Off road, baby motorcycle
5, Mini Tractor
6, Generator ; pump, engine
7, Outboard engine
8, CNG Track,CNG taxi Car CNG Bus.

If you have large order, we will help training your engineer. We wish to search factory to assemble above products in your country.

Looking forward to your reply!

Best regards,

Mr.Lee

(On Another Note) In a move that appears to be nothing other than colossal stupidity (or perhaps "free market" forces, which frequently boil down to the same thing), Chinese leadership has decided that China will begin to emulate the West in its autocentric ways. Bicycle traffic will be swept off many main streets to make room for cars. Not only does this seem foolish from a safety standpoint (there are more than two and a half times as many auto-related deaths in China than in the United States despite there being far fewer cars), but it also brings China into a tense strategic position of needing to protect its access to world oil reserves.

letter from spain

Hi, my name is Felipe Buitrago. I'm a 30 year old photographer addicted to bicycles. Born in Atlanta, Georgia, but living in Madrid, Spain for more than 15 years now.

I ran into your site through a link from Dennis' fixed gear gallery *(www.fixedgeargallery.com)*. I just wanted to let you know that I think your web page is an excellent idea. I've already forwarded your site to all of my friends and family. I've taken the liberty to translate your multiple reasons for riding a bike to Spanish adding a little translator's note due to cultural differences. And with your permission I would like to distribute them among the people of Madrid. I'm a firm believer in all the points which you express and being an ex-bike messenger and having been hit broadside by a 150cc scooter that went through a red light doing 55mph in the city, ending up in the hospital, and not seeing a penny for it - I didn't even have my bike paid for - makes me even more eager to illustrate the good things about bike riding. Madrid is a brutal place to ride, but I'll be damned if I'm going to let anyone take riding away from me.

Thanks for your time and good luck!

Ride On,

Felipe

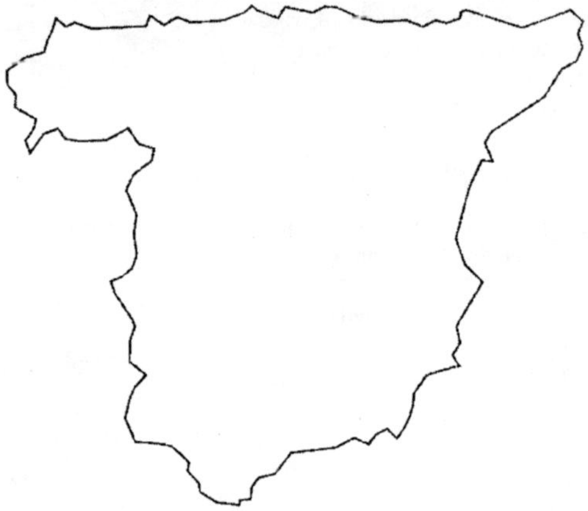

A few months after receiving this email, bombs exploded in a Madrid train station, killing nearly 200 people and injuring hundreds more. Adjusted for population, this would be the equivalent of about 1,400 American deaths, which is why some call March 11th Spain's September 11th.

The bombing was retaliation for Spanish leadership's willingness to kowtow to the most dominant military power in the history of the world, the United States. Despite Spanish popular opposition to the war, Spain (meaning the leadership) determined it would be better to appease the US. The bombing was timed before elections, and the Spanish people overwhelmingly voted for the socialist party which immediately withdrew all Spanish troops from Iraq. The Spanish people were so overwhelmingly opposed to the war before it started that sending troops to Iraq was an insult to Spanish democracy.

Iraq produces more oil than any other country except Saudi Arabia. The Bushes are a major Texas oil family. Dick Cheney was CEO of Halliburton, the world's largest oil service corporation. Condoleezza Rice was a director at Chevron from 1991 until she was appointed to the Bush administration in 2001. She has an oil tanker named after her. *Ride a bike.*

from hither and nither

The so-called "happiest place on earth," Disneyland, has one immediately noticeable difference from the city and region that surrounds it. There is no car traffic whatsoever.

"I would like to be part of building a model community, a City of Tomorrow, you might say, because I don't believe in going out to this extreme blue-sky stuff that some architects do. I believe that people still want to live like human beings. There's a lot of things that could be done. I'm not against the automobile, but I just feel that the automobile has moved into communities too much. I feel that you can design so that the automobile is there, but still put people back as pedestrians again, you see. I'd love to work on a project like that. ·

Walt Disney in 1965

Here are actual projections of cumulative impact, 2000 to 2020, if freight railroads stall: About 900 million tons of freight will shift onto the roads; cost to shippers will rise $326 billion; taxpayers will be charged $21 billion to $40 billion in extra highway and bridge upgrades; cost to highway users -- in travel time, accidents, operating costs -- will rise $492 billion.

Do these figures come from the rail lines? No! They were put together by two highly regarded transportation consulting teams (Cambridge Systematics, Reebie Associates). And they're published by the group long considered the top voice for expanded road building in the United States -- the American Association of State Highway and Transportation Officials (AASHTO).

Neal Peirce, Washington Post Writers Group, 16 March 2004

Mega-projects are large oil extractions which must be found yearly in order to meet demand.

If we look beyond 2007, however, the outlook becomes rather more problematic. Only three mega-projects are so far known for 2007 and a further three for 2008. For 2009 and 2010 only the later stages of existing projects are currently known about. Consequently, the volumes of new production (of oil) for this period are well below likely requirements.

Petroleum Review, January 2004

Reducing our addiction to automobiles is paramount, and the most effective way to do this is to curb sprawl and make our cities more compact and friendlier to walkers, cyclists, and mass transit. We've already made progress in this area -- witness the dramatic downtown growth and effective farmland protection policies of Vancouver, B.C. -- but we need to implement other innovations, such as zoning and tax measures that do a better job of encouraging mixed-use neighborhoods and modest increases of density, and that better enforce our urban growth boundaries.

Grist Magazine, 19 august 2003

Those who oppose war in Iraq must work together to prevent the conflicts that will follow if we fail to tackle car dependency. We must reclaim the streets, promote walking and cycling, strengthen public transport, oppose new road construction and pay the full social cost of car use. We must argue for land-use policies that reduce the need for car travel. We need "urban villages" clustered around public transport nodes, not sprawling car-dependent conurbations. We can all play our part and we must act now.

quoted from a Guardian editorial, 18 January 2003

Despite the improvements in the last decade, federal transportation policy is overwhelmingly geared towards road-building, with $4 spent on highways for every $1 spent on public transit. From 1998 to 2003, federal funding for highways increased by more than 40%, while traffic congestion has continued to worsen, particularly in urban areas.

The American Highway Users Alliance (AHUA), a large trade association representing car manufacturers, contractors, developers and other corporations with financial stake in highway construction, argues that the solution is to build more roads, even at the expense of transit and other alternative forms of transportation. In recent years, however, scholars and an increasing numbers of transportation planners have come to realize that building new roads actually spurs vehicle travel, creating new traffic.

Extending a highway into a new area effectively opens that area to large-scale development, often of the sprawling, auto-dependent variety. Meanwhile the expansion of highway capacity can speed travel times to allow drivers to take more or longer trips in the same amount of time or even encourage those who had shifted to other modes of transportation to return to driving. The end product of these decisions is more vehicle travel, a phenomenon know as "generated traffic."

U.S. Pirg report entitled "More Highways, More Pollution."

In Sweden, a decision was made to change the driving from the left side of the road to the right side in order to match the rest of continental Europe. After this decision was adopted and implemented, car crashes dropped by 17 percent, which seems counter intuitive. Slowly over the next several months, crashes steadily increased until they were at the same level that they were before the change was put in place.

The obvious interpretation of this phenomenon is that when drivers slow down and pay more attention rather than driving habitually, the rate of crashes decreases and makes it safer for pedestrians, bicyclists and other drivers.

Along these same lines, intersections that are very confusing and replete with obstacles always have lower rates of crashes because drivers slow down and pay attention. Because of the relative low speed of bicycling (not to mention better visibility), the chances of accidents are decreased even further, and cities that promote cycling are by their very nature more safe for everyone.

Paraphrased from *Suburban Nation*

andy singer

Andy Singer's cartoons have appeared just about everywhere that transportation is concerned. He has used his sharp wit to attack a mode of transportation that has been forcefed to the American public for decades. At the same time he shows us the options and how they far surpass the personal automobile in safety, community and economics.

For more information, visit **www.andysinger.com** where you will find more cartoons about transportation and other subjects. His transportation cartoons are collected into a volume called, appropriately enough, CARtoons. It is available from **carbusters.org** and **akpress.org**.

tom lechner

At the 2003 Portland Zine Symposium, I bought a copy of Tom Lechner's zine called *Bicycle Propaganda*. I thought the title of his zine was an odd one.

The connotations of the word *propaganda* are without a doubt negative. It is something which is sinister and manipulative, created for diabolical purposes. I thought that someone picking up Lechner's zine for the first time may be biased towards it because of these associations, even if on an unconscious level.

But the word *propaganda* did not always have these associations. Only after the second World War, when it started to be associated with the Nazis, did the word lose its neutrality. Before and during the war it was used quite freely in the United States to describe information whose purpose was to influence thoughts, emotions and behaviors.

When you see an ad on television for a new SUV, it is called advertising, and when corporations reach out to the public with campaigns it is called public relations, which both are pure Orwellian euphemism. Despite the euphemisms, both instances are propaganda nonetheless.

After pondering it for a while, I saw Lechner's title as perfect. Not because he is promoting something sinister, but because the title is completely honest. Like technology, propaganda can be used for both benign and malignant purposes. With his advocacy of a sensible and sustainable mode of transportation, Lechner is certainly working towards something benign.

To find out more or to order copies, visit **www.re.org/tom**. Copies are also currently available at both Citybikes locations in Southeast Portland. Lechner also self-publishes Consumption, a zine critical of world politics and big business, which has made me laugh out loud several times.

nothing aggravates the willingly subjugated
more than non-conformity